Minds in Connection

The Legacy of Mary Ainsworth

Freudian Trips

Copyright Page

Disclaimer

The views and opinions expressed in this book are those of
the author(s) and do not necessarily reflect the official policy
or position of any other agency, organization, employer, or
company. The contents of this book are for informational and
educational purposes only and are not intended to serve as
professional advice, diagnosis, or treatment.

The information provided in this book is believed to be
accurate and reliable as of the date of publication. However, it
may include some errors or inaccuracies, and no warranty or
guarantee is provided regarding the accuracy, timeliness, or
applicability of the content.

Readers are encouraged to consult with professional
philosophers, educators, or other qualified professionals
where appropriate for personalized advice. The author(s) and
publisher shall not be liable for any loss, damage, or harm
caused or alleged to be caused, directly or indirectly, by the

information or ideas contained, suggested, or referenced in this book.

By reading this book, the reader acknowledges and agrees that they are solely responsible for how they interpret and apply the information contained herein.

This book may also include references to other works, studies, and sources. These references are provided for further reading and exploration and do not imply endorsement or validation of the specific theories, viewpoints, or interpretations presented in those works.

Introduction: The Invisible Ties that Shape Us

Imagine a young child. Maybe they're laughing gleefully with a parent, or perhaps they're crying inconsolably because a beloved toy is missing. What we don't always see are the hidden threads between that child and the most important people in their world. These threads are called attachment.

Attachment is an invisible bond that forms in a baby's earliest moments. It's a deep connection to a special adult who makes them feel safe, loved, and understood. This bond isn't just about having someone to feed or clothe them. It's the foundation upon which a child builds their whole sense of the world and how they fit within it.

Before a woman named Mary Ainsworth came along, the science of childhood was quite different. Many experts thought of babies mainly as bundles of basic needs – feed them, keep them warm, and they'll thrive. They didn't focus much on the emotional relationships babies have with their caregivers.

Ainsworth's path to changing all of this was unusual. Born in the United States, her life took a dramatic turn when a chance encounter with a book by famous psychologist William Blatz inspired a deep interest in how children's minds work. Her experiences serving in World War II, where she saw the deep impact of families separated by conflict, further fueled her passion.

Ainsworth wasn't content to just read about how children develop. She bravely moved to Uganda, Africa, to directly observe families in a very different culture from her own. This broadened her horizons and made her question the assumptions of many Western experts about children.

These adventures shaped Ainsworth into a scientist who looked beyond just the surface. She knew there were powerful forces at work beneath a child's tears or smiles. Her challenge was to find a way to reveal these hidden connections and prove just how important they really are.

Chapter 1: Seeds of Curiosity

Mary Ainsworth's story doesn't begin in a laboratory, but a small town in Ohio. She was the first of three daughters in a book-loving family. Her parents valued knowledge, and their home was filled with stories. This love of learning became a defining part of who Mary would become.

As a young woman, Mary followed her passion for understanding the mind to the University of Toronto. It was here that a chance encounter changed everything. A dusty book by a psychologist named William Blatz fell into her hands. Blatz didn't just theorize about how children develop, he talked about security – the feeling of being truly safe and supported as a foundation for growth. This concept struck a deep chord in Mary.

Blatz became her mentor, encouraging her unique blend of curiosity and compassion. She wasn't just interested in facts and figures; she wanted to understand how children felt inside, what truly made them thrive.

Then, history intervened. World War II erupted, drawing Mary away from her studies. She joined the Canadian Women's Army Corps, rising through the ranks. This wasn't about book knowledge anymore. She was counseling soldiers and their families, seeing the real-world heartbreak caused when loved ones were lost or separated.

The war didn't break her spirit. Instead, it deepened her determination. If deep bonds could be damaged in adults by conflict, what effect might separation and loss have on a young, vulnerable child? The puzzle pieces were starting to come together, leading Mary toward a quest that would define her career.

Chapter 2: Eyes Wide Open in Africa

After the war, Mary was ready for a new adventure. Imagine how bold she must have been—a young woman leaving behind all she knew to journey to Uganda, Africa. This wasn't a typical research trip for the time, especially not for a woman on her own.

Mary had an important goal. She teamed up with John Bowlby, a British doctor who was also fascinated by how early experiences shape children. Bowlby believed that babies weren't just driven by hunger or basic needs—they had an intense need to feel connected to their caregivers for survival. Mary wanted to see this in action.

In Uganda, Mary didn't just sit in a lab. She went to villages, lived among families, and watched. She paid attention to the tiny details, the little moments that most Western experts overlooked: how mothers soothed a crying baby, how children played and explored, how they reacted when a parent left and came back.

What she saw began to challenge the "rules" set by many child development researchers of the time. In the West, mothers were often told to keep a bit of distance, not to spoil their babies by picking them up every time they cried. But in Uganda, mothers seemed deeply in tune with their babies, responding quickly and warmly. Yet, these children weren't overly clingy, they were confident and curious!

Mary began to realize that there's no single "right" way to be a parent. Different cultures have different customs. But what seemed universal was the need for that core bond – a safe haven child could always come back to. These observations fueled her passion and laid the groundwork for her most famous work back in the United States.

Chapter 3: The Room Where Secrets Were Revealed

Returning to America, Mary Ainsworth was a woman on a mission. She was determined to prove that the invisible emotional bonds children have with their caregivers weren't just a nice idea; they were crucial to healthy development. But how do you measure something as delicate as a feeling?

Getting a chance to do this research wasn't easy. Science at the time was mostly a man's world, and many didn't take seriously the idea that babies' feelings mattered all that much. Mary persevered, eventually landing a position at Johns Hopkins University in Baltimore.

Now, she had to figure out an experiment. It couldn't just be a questionnaire – she needed to watch real parent-child interactions. She came up with a clever plan called the "Strange Situation." Picture a simple playroom. A mother and baby enter, there are toys to explore. Then, a friendly stranger comes in. The mother leaves briefly, then returns.

It sounds simple, but this short sequence was a stroke of genius. It created just enough gentle stress to reveal how the baby truly felt about their mom. Did they cry with worry when she left? Were they overjoyed upon her return, seeking comfort? Or did they act like they barely noticed?

Mary carefully observed hundreds of these interactions. Patterns started to emerge:

- **Secure Attachment:** These babies used their mom as a "secure base." They explored happily, might be upset by her leaving, but were visibly soothed when she returned.
- **Insecure-Avoidant:** These babies seemed aloof, not too upset when mom left, and didn't seek much comfort when she returned. It was like they'd learned to mask their feelings.
- **Insecure-Ambivalent:** These babies were very clingy and upset when mom left, but hard to soothe upon her return. They seemed both to need her and to be angry at the same time.

Mary had done it! She revealed the hidden patterns of attachment, proving that what happens in those earliest moments of life leaves a lasting imprint.

Chapter 4: From the Playroom to the Real World

Mary Ainsworth wasn't the kind of scientist who just published findings and moved on. She knew her work had the power to change lives. The Strange Situation didn't just make for interesting charts and graphs - it held a mirror up to society.

Suddenly, parents had a new way to think about their role. It wasn't just about feeding, bathing, and keeping their child safe from physical harm. They were also their child's emotional safe haven. Ainsworth emphasized the importance of "maternal sensitivity" – not perfect parenting, but being able to tune in to your baby's signals and respond with warmth and understanding.

This message resonated. Daycare centers started rethinking their policies. Were they providing enough loving connection and not just a place to park children while parents worked? Doctors and therapists found a new lens to understand troubled children. Had something disrupted their early attachments, and could that be addressed in therapy?

Ainsworth's insights even stretched beyond childhood. Think about how you act in your adult romantic relationships. Are you secure, trusting that your partner will be there for you? Or perhaps a bit anxious, fearing they might leave? Or maybe you keep people at arm's length, afraid of getting hurt. Turns out, the way you learned to connect as a baby can leave echoes throughout your life.

The Strange Situation wasn't a magic solution for every problem. But it opened a door. It showed that the love and attention we give (or don't give) children in those earliest years shapes them more deeply than we often realize. That's a powerful message for parents, caregivers, and for anyone who's ever been a child.

Chapter 5: Questions and Challenges

Mary Ainsworth's work was groundbreaking, but breakthroughs often bring debate. Like any scientific theory, attachment theory didn't answer every question perfectly, and it faced some fair challenges.

One big question was: Are these patterns of attachment the same everywhere in the world? Ainsworth's journey to Africa showed her that different cultures express love in different ways. But could those differences mean a child who seems "avoidant" in a Western setting might be showing a different kind of security in another culture? Critics felt the Strange Situation might have a built-in bias.

Another concern centered on the whole setup of the experiment – it's a bit artificial. Real life is messy, and maybe a short lab test couldn't truly capture the richness of a parent-child bond. Plus, the Strange Situation mostly looked at how babies reacted to mothers briefly leaving, but what about fathers? Couldn't they be just as important for a child's sense of security?

Ainsworth acknowledged some of these limitations. She was a careful scientist, always open to new information. Her work didn't mean dads don't matter, nor that every child everywhere fits neatly into those original three categories.

What made her work so powerful was that it sparked more questions! Later researchers dug deeper into cultural differences, the role of fathers, and how early experiences interact with a child's unique temperament. Science builds upon itself, and Ainsworth provided a strong foundation.

Chapter 6: The Ripple Effects

Mary Ainsworth's greatest legacy might not be the discovery of the attachment types themselves, but the way she ignited a fire of curiosity. Her work proved that those early bonds were worth a closer look, leading to decades of exciting research that deepened our understanding.

Scientists started asking bolder questions. What if a child's experiences aren't just "good enough" for secure attachment, but actively harmful? A new category emerged: "Disorganized Attachment." These children often experienced frightening or unpredictable behavior from their caregivers, and in the Strange Situation, they seemed confused, unable to find comfort. This discovery highlighted the need for interventions to protect children in truly troubled family situations.

Ainsworth's focus on mothers sparked important conversations about other caregivers. Dads, grandparents, and even quality daycare providers proved to be vital in shaping children's sense of security. Attachment wasn't about one special parent only, but a network of love and support.

Perhaps most importantly, attachment theory moved out of the lab and into the lives of children and families. Therapists learned to look beyond just a child's current behavior, searching for clues about past experiences that might be causing struggles. Social workers began focusing on supporting parents and building strong attachments, rather than only reacting to situations when they had already gone wrong.

Mary Ainsworth helped us see that the emotional needs of children aren't a luxury, they're a necessity. Her legacy is a world a little more understanding, a little more compassionate, and a little more attuned to the amazing power of those first invisible bonds of love.

Chapter 7: The Bonds That Shape Our World

Think for a moment about how differently we see children now compared to a few decades ago. It might seem obvious that babies need love, but that wasn't always the focus. Mary Ainsworth played a huge part in changing that.

Parents today have way more access to information about the importance of emotional connection with their little ones. We understand that picking up a crying baby isn't spoiling them, it's building trust. We have a language to talk about things like 'attunement' and 'responsiveness,' thanks to researchers like Ainsworth.

Her impact is in our classrooms, too. Teachers are trained in social-emotional development, not just academics. They watch out for signs that a child may be struggling with insecure attachment, perhaps due to difficult experiences at home, so they can get support.

Ainsworth's work even changed how we view ourselves. Many adults who struggle with difficult relationships or low self-esteem wonder, "Did something happen in my childhood to make me feel this way?". Attachment theory offers a potential lens, without offering simplistic blame. It's opened up possibilities for healing and growth at any age.

The science of attachment continues to evolve. We know more about the brain, how trauma impacts children, and about the different ways people express their emotions across cultures. But the core idea that Ainsworth championed remains powerful: love is essential.

The bonds we form in our earliest days cast a long shadow. They influence how secure we feel in the world, how we connect with others, how we cope with stress. Mary Ainsworth helped reveal these invisible threads, giving us tools to weave them into stronger, more compassionate families, communities, and a kinder world for the next generation.

Conclusion: A Legacy of Love

Mary Ainsworth wasn't a woman who sought fame. She wanted to understand children, to make a difference. In that, she achieved extraordinary success. Her journey teaches us that groundbreaking science can come from looking beyond the obvious, from paying attention to the quiet moments between a baby and a parent.

Her greatest gift was revealing the extraordinary in the ordinary. The simple act of a mother soothing a crying child isn't insignificant. It's the building block of a healthy mind, a strong heart, and a sense of security that allows that child to explore the world with confidence.

The story of attachment theory doesn't end with Ainsworth, of course. Her work sparked a chain reaction of questions and discoveries. We're likely to learn even more about how temperament and experience interact, about the unique challenges faced by adopted children or those in foster care, and about how to help repair broken attachments at any age.

Perhaps one day, society will fully support parents in those precious early years, with generous leave policies and quality childcare that prioritizes emotional connection just as much as learning. Imagine the impact on future generations if every child had the best possible start for forming secure, loving bonds.

Mary Ainsworth would likely be both humbled by the influence of her work and impatient for us to do even more. The science continues, but the heart of her message remains timeless: love is not just a feeling, it's an act of nurturing the next generation. Whether you're a parent, an educator, a policymaker, or simply someone hoping for a more compassionate world, her legacy reminds us that it all begins with the bonds we build.

About Freudian Trips

Welcome to Freudian Trips, your dedicated platform for diving deep into the world of psychology. We are more than just a YouTube channel or a book publisher. We are a beacon of enlightenment, making complex psychological concepts accessible and engaging for all.

Our YouTube channel is a rich repository of psychology made simple. We take the profound and often complex ideas from the world of psychology and break them down into digestible, easy-to-understand content. From the foundational theories of Freud to the cognitive insights of Piaget, we cover a broad spectrum of psychological schools and thoughts, making psychology accessible to everyone, regardless of their background or prior knowledge.

As a book publisher, we take the same approach, transforming intricate psychological theories into comprehensible narratives. Our books are not just collections of words, but vessels of wisdom that make psychology approachable and relatable. We believe that psychology should not be confined to academic circles, but should be available to all who seek to understand the human mind and behavior.

At Freudian Trips, we believe in the power of curiosity and the pursuit of knowledge. We are here to stoke the fires of your curiosity, to guide you on your intellectual journey, and to help you navigate the fascinating world of psychology.

If you are someone who is not afraid to question, to explore, and to learn, then you are in the right place. Join us on this journey of exploration, as we make psychology easy to understand, one concept at a time.

Be sure to visit our Youtube channel at:
www.freudiantrips.com/youtube

You can also visit us on the web at www.freudiantrips.com

Welcome to The Freudian Trip community. Stay curious. Stay enlightened.